Letters of Love to the World from a Dark Man

By Charles Clark

Charles Clark

First Edition. Copyright © 2025 by Charles Clark

All rights reserved. No part of this publication may be reproduced, distributed, or transmitted in any form or by any means, including photocopying, recording, or other electronic or mechanical methods, without the prior written permission of the publisher.

For permissions, contact cpcenterpries@gmail.com

DEDICATION

This book is dedicated to my parents, **Charles and Carlean Clark**, and to my son, **Zarko Lance Ellis Jr.**

My father lived to be 90.
My mother lived to be 80.
My son passed at just 30 years old—a young, vibrant man who loved everyone he met.

Each of them shaped my life in ways I can never repay.
I love them deeply. May they rest in peace.

Charles Clark

THE LOVE LETTERS

INTRODUCTION 5
LOVE 6
SEX 15
DRUGS 28
VIOLENCE 33
WAR 40
DEATH 44
RELIGION 50
THE BIBLE 59
GOD 70
THE MESSAGE 78
CONCLUSION 83

Letters of Love to the World from a Dark Man

INTRODUCTION

COLORED

We are all colored differently, from beige to brown. Just open your eyes and look around—we are more the same than people think. Don't judge me harshly because my skin is not pink. We all need love to help us live. We must forgive the mistakes of the past. We will all be judged—and seen as the same—by the one we call by His holy name. Color will not matter on judgment day. So love all of God's people in every way.

ME

We are all the same color in the dark. Can you tell what color I am, being named Clark? Come out of the dark and see the light. The proclivity of people is to have blind sight—not looking objectively at whom they see, but only seeing what they want to see. Rose-colored glasses make the day look good; when you take them off, things look different, as they should. Feel the pain and suffering of being me. The façade I project is all people see.

Charles Clark

LOVE

Love of all things is the greatest because God is love. This book is about love letters. These letters are to you—the people who read this book. The love of God is the greatest love. God loves all of us. God has given us life.

Life is also a fight.

Many years ago, when I was a young man—no! A boy—I made childish decisions. I was pro-abortion because I used abortion as a form of birth control. When I was 18, I had a few ladies pregnant. I had one miscarriage at six months, one tubal pregnancy, and one abortion. She came to me and told me we could not afford a baby. "I don't want to be a teenage mom. Let's get rid of 'it.'" "IT" was my child. In the passing years, it occurred several more times. Of course, being the prick I was, I said, "Let's get rid of it." It—in all my cases, they were my children. My children.

To this day, I have no biological children. If anyone out there kept one of my "its," please let me know. Please

Letters of Love to the World from a Dark Man

forgive me. Over the years, this has been the most difficult thing in my life—to forgive myself. God gives us a gift from heaven, and we tear it out and throw it in a wastebasket. If any of you have been through the "it" syndrome, I hope that you have forgiven yourself. God forgives, but we humans have a problem forgiving ourselves. We commit crimes against ourselves.

This chapter is about love, but in order to have love, we have to not hate. I believe that the woman has the right to do what she wants to do with her body, but give me my baby. As years went by, I begged for the lives of my children because I realized the mistakes that I had made. God made sex for procreation, not for pleasure. We have taken it to the next level—pleasure: S&M, one-night stands, sodomy, fornication, adultery, rape, STDs, porn, strip clubs, escorts, gigolos, pimps, and prostitutes.

God meant for it to be one man and one woman for life. I am your thug for life. If a woman sleeps with a man who is hung like a horse and only with him for life, she does not know anything different. She thinks that all men are that big and her body conforms to his. That is the way God planned it. Another woman marries a man that has dwarf cock syndrome, and they are both virgins by the same token. She is satisfied and has many children for him. She thinks he is hung like a horse also. In our sexually active society, how many people are virgins when they get married? Very few pass the test.

People call it "making love." If God is love, then should we say "Let's make God"? Are we that far removed from God that God is not part of our everyday life—the life that God gave us? In life, we have the potential to do anything we want. So the next time you have sex, why don't you say, "Let's make God," because you cannot make God! God has made you. He is the creator. God has made love. God made love when he made everything. His love is displayed throughout the universe. He shines through every time a child is born—a bundle of joy. A bundle of love is a product of lovemaking.

Love is many splendid things: love hurts, love stinks, lovesick, puppy love, love hangover, love cures everything, love is timeless, and love is in the air. Let us deal with these last three.

Love cures everything. Once again, our postulate is that God is love, then God can cure everything, which he can. This is manifested by the miracles of Jesus Christ and the other works of God. Even today when a miracle occurs, it shows that God is in control. God's love cures anything and anybody.

Letters of Love to the World from a Dark Man

Love is timeless. Of course it is, because God is love, and we all know that God is timeless. God is not bound by our earthly measures of time. God is only bound by God. God is not bound by time or space because God is everywhere, and God is God all the time. God is the eternal timekeeper—the alpha and the omega. As we simple humans are bound by time, even if you live to be 120 years old, that is nothing compared to eternity. God is eternity. Never-ending time and never-ending love. Endless love!

Last, but not least, "**Love is in the air.**" Substitute "God" for "Love" and you have "God is in the air." God is not only in the air—God is the air. What can we do without breathing? No breath, no life. We take our last breath. No God, no life. God gives us so much love.

We talk about loving ourselves, loving others, and loving God. But how many people love things and jobs when they speak of love? We have to love God above all. For all you job lovers out there, you better come to your senses. You are the "go-to person," the irreplaceable employee, the boss! When you get sick, die, or get fired by the job that needed you so much, they will find a replacement. When Willie B died at the Atlanta zoo, they found another gorilla! Your job does not need or love you that much!

Love your family. The people at your job may care about you. The people at the job may love you. We spend more time with the people at work than we do with our families at home. The institution that you work for is a machine—it is a system of cogs and sprockets. One part goes bad, they replace it with another one. That is why it is called a system.

People, on the other hand, are capable of emotion. Love is an emotion—you cannot put it in a box, touch it, or see it. You can see the manifestations of love: gifts, bonds, and relationships. We manifest our love through our relationships. Even at our jobs, we work through people and our relationships. The church—the people are the church. We have relationships. Our families are relatives, which comes from relations—we have relationships. We also have a relationship with God. Let's not forget our relationships with animals and nature.

Therefore, you could love the people at work. I do not recommend falling in love with people at work. Many people find love at the workplace because, as I stated earlier, you spend at least one-third of your day at work. I also have worked as a nurse and spent half of my day at work because we work 12-hour shifts. There is no set boundary for relationships. They are as convoluted as quantum physics. Whatever works for you—if you can

Letters of Love to the World from a Dark Man

put up with it, it's fine by me. Go right ahead. If you like it, I love it!

The problem with relationships at work is: what happens if you break up? You have to see the same person that used to be intimate with you and still remain professional. People have affairs at work, and in nursing it happens all the time—doctors and nurses, nurses and nurses, CNAs and doctors, and all the rest of the ancillary staff. It goes down in the hospital. Yeah, some people find love anywhere. That is contingent on the level of commitment of the individuals. Some people can work together, sleep together—some people can do everything together and make it work. A play on words, but as for the rest of us, buyer beware.

Love is everywhere. I hope you find it, but it begins with you. To have a lover, you have to be a lover first. Even in our relationship with God, we have to love ourselves. You cannot hate yourself—self-hate condemns us to death, spiritual death. You cannot love your neighbors as yourself if you hate you! Everything in life starts with you! God loves you because he gave you life. Love God by loving him back and loving yourself. Then and only then can the rest of the world love you.

The church is like the original church—the church is a

group of people. How much time do you spend with your church? As for pastors and people who are called to do God's work all the time, once again, the love of God is the greatest love of all. Do we spend as much time at church as we do at work? No way! One or two hours on Sunday, a few hours on Wednesday. Let's go highball and say 10 hours a week at church, compared to 40 hours a week at work. Now are we talking about the building or the people? Aha! The people, of course.

We all have sick church members that need food, but many of the shut-ins just need your time and your love. So many elderly people have told me that they died of loneliness—feeling afraid and not loved. Reach out with your hand to those who need it most. That is what an Outreach Ministry is. Reach out, outreach—don't keep your hands by your side. You have to open up your arms and your hearts in order to hug someone. Did you hug someone today? I did. I try to hug at least someone every day. Touch everyone. In our germophobic society, we are veering away from touch. People do not touch each other as much as they used to.

The people of the original church were not Christians. They were not Catholics. They were not all Jews. They were called the people of "The Way." Outsiders called them this because of the way they loved each other. They

Letters of Love to the World from a Dark Man

treated each other so well, like Jesus is the way, the truth, and the life.

Church people, the next time you start some mess at the building, think about the way you should treat people.

Christianity has spread and subdivided into over 200 different sects. There are hundreds of different religions, but there is only one God. Find your way! Do you see the light? The truth. Man seeks the truth—find it for yourself. This chapter is about love. Be the light before you see the light!

Our families are important. The basic unit of society has always been the family. Once again, my thoughts are that loving your family is like loving yourself. Is the greatest love of all learning to love yourself? Perhaps. "I just wanna be loved and needed, depended on to give love, love I can't give when you're gone."

This is a quote from one of my favorite songs. Is our ability to give love contingent on other people being there? That may be true for some people. The greatest love of all is the love of God, then learning to love yourself is next, because God loved me first. Well, there you have it.

The most dynamic, powerful relationship we have is our

relationship with God. All things we talk about go full circle and back to God. God has loved us all first. Therefore, our love for God is where it all starts and where it all ends. We should never overlook the importance of God in our lives. Love God, praise God. God first, and everything else will fall in line.

The whole message in this book is that **God is love. Love is all we need.** By Joe, I think I've got it! So many songs have been written about love throughout history. If God equals love, then all you need is God.

Letters of Love to the World from a Dark Man

SEX

Sex—one of my favorite subjects. This may be one of the shortest chapters in my book. We tend to avoid the issue of sex in the USA. The degree of sexual repression in this country goes back to its roots. In Europe, there are breasts everywhere—the beach, magazines, and other places.

When Americans travel abroad, they go to the beaches and stare at women's breasts. The men wear speedos, which show everything. The magazines in certain European countries have nudity. I remember when I was young, studying French back in the 70s, I thought that Match De Paris was a soft porn magazine. We used to stare at the nudity.

In the 70s, we were in the era of sexual freedom in the United States. You could pick up a person and go and copulate and have nothing to worry about—no herpes, no AIDS, no chlamydia. You might catch the clap, but all you needed was a dose of penicillin, which was accessible. In the early 80s, herpes attacked. People were talking about people who had cold sores on their lips. It was the herpes. People thought it was bad—at least if you got genital herpes, no one could see it. Eventually people accepted herpes; nobody cares about it nowadays. People want herpes; it's better than AIDS.

Then in the late 80s and early 90s, AIDS came out. No one knew where it came from or what to do about it. People thought: How is it passed? Casual contact? Or close contact? What type of disease is it? Is it a punishment for the sexual revolution? Is it God's wrath against a promiscuous society? Why did this disease have to come about? Only God knows.

I am a research chemist by trade. I graduated from Georgia State University in 1993. One of my many projects that I was working on was finding a cure for AIDS. This research was in conjunction with Emory University and the CDC. The focus of the research was simply identifying AIDS—at that point, we were so concerned with false positives. We were working on the variance between the Western blot method versus the ELISA assay. The research at that time said that the Western blot was more reliable. Today's research backs that up.

AIDS has changed the sex game. People are less likely to have unprotected sex or one-night stands than back in the

Letters of Love to the World from a Dark Man

day. Research today says that there is a difference between HIV and AIDS. I believe that there is no difference. Years ago, people believed that AIDS had a possible incubation period of 8 to 10 years. We know better than that today. If a person is possibly infected, then there is about a 30-minute window that you can start them on antiviral medications to combat the proliferation of the disease. This medical regimen goes on for at least a year with monthly follow-up testing.

For those who are not able to identify the virus that early, it is many times diagnosed during a routine blood test—like many people have when applying for a marriage license or any other routine blood test that may be taken in a hospital visit or doctor's office appointment. Certain famous individuals have acquired HIV and live with it nowadays, but many years ago it was considered a death sentence. Certain people nowadays have even put on weight being on HIV and AIDS medications. Years ago, there was a certain look for most AIDS patients. They were considered to be thin and unhealthy. Many people called them "HIVers with the shivers" because a lot of people got fevers back then. They would come to the hospital shaking.

People are living longer with the disease now. Most people with AIDS or HIV-positive individuals tell people about their malady prior to being intimate. But there are some people who don't want to tell possible sexual partners that they have HIV or AIDS because they want to spread the virus as payback to the world for getting them infected. What a shame.

The spread of the disease in this country was heightened when married men were having homosexual relationships with other men and then bringing it home to their wives. These men were called "low-low," "down low," and "flippers." The titles are self-explanatory.

A "low-low" is like a "down low"—they keep it undercover and portray a life that they are totally straight because they are married.

A "flipper" is one that switches back and forth, commonly known as bisexual. Most bisexual people are open about their sexuality.

People are constantly having sex and changing partners. If you must do that, wrap it up and get tested. Everything that looks good might not be good for you.

The sexual revolution of the 70s was changed in the 80s by drugs and strip clubs. Let us explore the emergence of these two entities. There were drugs in the 70s, but when

Letters of Love to the World from a Dark Man

cocaine took the front stage from marijuana, which increased the transition from cocaine to freebase to crack, Mary Jane—which was the feel-good starter kit drug—took a backseat. Of course, you had some people who didn't do drugs, but the majority of the population did some form of stress relief. Alcohol and tobacco are drugs too. Prescription pain medications are drugs too.

In the 70s, cocaine was considered to be a designer drug for rich people. People did acid and speed during the 70s, and it lingered on into the 80s, but most people smoked marijuana. Heroin was there, but it was more of a 60s drug and early 70s drug. Some of the Vietnam veterans returning from overseas were addicted to heroin. Poppy seeds transcended the oceans and gathered a nice group of people with the serious slows. "Hopheads" had puffy hands from tying off their arms. They seemed like coke heads when they were out doing whatever it took to get a fix.

Cocaine, on the other hand, was different. You could not smell it; it did not make you feel silly like weed. It was a businessman's drug. It gave you an air of confidence, made you a little quicker on your feet, and didn't have such a big crash if done in moderation. Cocaine became affordable in about 1982. You could get a gram of cocaine for about $125-$150. That is not a cheap buzz, but for a birthday or special occasion, it was cool. Most people only did it every once in a while. Weed at that time was about $100 an ounce. It might last a real weed head about a week. Some people could make that ounce last a month. So the price difference made weed more affordable. One hundred dollars was a lot for a one-day buzz.

Then freebase came about, which was the predecessor to crack. People pooled their money to play "baseball." There would usually be someone in the room called "the cook." The cook would take all of the powder and re-rock it. The process involved cooking the product down in a glass heat-resistant dish until it dissolved. Once it dissolved, they would run cold water on the vial and swirl it around. The final product would appear.

It was dope boy magic. This was pure, uncut cocaine with all of the impurities washed out. This was "the rock." The cook usually took the first hit. They were baseball players: "It's your hit." Some people would pass out from one hit on the pipe. They called that "a blast." Some people died from one hit. Their heart couldn't take the blast. Other people became addicted to the strong drug after one hit.

Why am I spending so much time talking about drugs? Because this epidemic drew in a new wave of users.

Letters of Love to the World from a Dark Man

Some of the new drug users were women who had never been caught up in the game before. They were gorgeous and held jobs for the most part, but some fell into crackhouse prostitution. The males at the dope house would put the pipe by their pipe and blow the smoke out in the ladies' faces. "You have to suck one to suck on the other." Of course, they would do it just to get another hit, many times doing this with multiple partners at the same time. Some of the drug dealers would sit at the drug houses and collect the money from the tricks, and the women would do anything just for another hit. That led the drug dealer into a new position of being a pimp too. This changed drugs and changed the streets because it almost put the pimps out of business.

What does all of this have to do with love?

This shows that there is a distinct dichotomy between sex and love. Love is an emotion that we feel. Intercourse itself is the most intimate interaction. Yet people take it for granted. People have discounted it. Some people love sex. Some people believe that drugs enhance the sexual experience. We all know that drugs increase the promiscuity of many individuals, and some people even use it as an excuse for actions that they did: "I was drunk when I did that." This is an excuse for actions that you knew you were participating in.

But the end result was there were people who in less than a year looked one way at the beginning of the year. By the end of the year, they looked like a classic crackhead. They were skinny. They had lost their front teeth—sometimes they were knocked out intentionally to make the fellatio better. Their body was run down by the streets. They had no place to sleep but the dope house. They lost everything. This epidemic hit many of the large cities so badly. Where is the love?

The next thing that changed the new sexual revolution was strip clubs. Strip clubs have been around before. Strip clubs are set up just like casinos—they don't have any windows or clocks. They have ATM machines, so you could never run out of cash. There are multiple ATMs in every strip club, and you are one of them! Therefore, you lose track of time and how much money you have spent. What a bargain!

But in the 1990s, they went to a new level. People actually began to fall in love with strippers. This change occurred because if you could not pull a pretty woman, you could pay your money to be with a dime piece for 3 to 5 minutes or until your money ran out. Magic City, Strokers, the Blue Flame, Jason's, the Brass Rail, the Diamond Club, Club Nikki, the Gold Club, the Cheetah,

Letters of Love to the World from a Dark Man

Flashers, Stormin Norman's, the Pink Pony, the Black Orchid, the Black Diamond, Dancers, the Gentleman's Club, Jazzy T's, the Purple Onion, Fantasy Island, and many other strip clubs redefined the two-drink and five-dollar steak lunch. You could have a five-dollar steak and two five-dollar cocktails while looking at a beautiful woman for lunch. And go home and jump on your wife, and she would wonder why you were so frisky. Some guys would go home and throw rocks at their wife. Most people keep the game in perspective.

The strippers had a perfect job. Stripping is legal; there's no sexual intercourse involved in it. This is a controlled environment. It has security and cameras everywhere. No touching—that's relative depending on what the dancer wants. If she wants to trick off, she can. Plus it gives her all types of advertisement for private parties and other endeavors. Many strippers have been featured in movies, on videos, on websites, and are millionaires. Many of the strippers will tell you, "I like women," and others went both ways. Some guys would actually date the strippers, but that was few and far between. To them it was a job; they enjoyed their job.

Some strippers would take flights out of town to strip in another city because they held down a regular job, or some of their families might be prominent in their hometown. Others were local talent. There was a group of strippers who were all college students. They considered this working their way through college, and many of them became successful businesswomen after they finished dancing and college. Some of the strippers stayed in the strip club until they became the house mom. They work the front door or just helped the girls get dressed in between changes.

If you had enough money, you could do whatever you wanted to in the strip club. There are drugs in strip clubs and drug dealers. A drug dealer can go and spend their cash anyway they want to, and there will be no questions asked of where you got it from. You had to pay like you weigh. There is also a strange phenomenon in strip clubs called "baller syndrome." This is when a group of people in the strip club are trying to show and spend more money than another group of people in the strip club to show who is the big baller. The winner, of course, is always the dancer.

Then men started bringing their girlfriends to the strip club. In general, the women would pick women that they thought that their boyfriend would like. Some would pick women that they liked. These couples would learn a lot about their relationship and true sexual preference. Suddenly groups of straight women would flock to the

Letters of Love to the World from a Dark Man

strip club. At first I didn't know, then I asked a lady, "Why are you here?" She said, "This is where the men are." By the end of the night, I saw her and her bunch of friends leave with a group of fellows. I saw this happen on multiple occasions.

One night I saw what I thought was two dudes with ten dancers in the back corner having a good time. I walked over there to check out the action. They dressed alike in Timberland boots, baggy jeans, sweatshirt, and caps. I got closer and saw that they had breasts. They were women. They were studs.

A lot of the strip clubs have private rooms downstairs or in the back. They call them VIP suites. There is usually a charge just to rent the room, and the price of the dances increases. This is where the sexual acts occurred. People were having protected and unprotected sex in the strip club. This also increased the epidemic of sexually transmitted diseases. Some strippers would have intercourse with five or six people in the course of a shift. Others would not cross that line. They said, "I am strictly a dancer."

Sometimes people would stalk them. There have been some famous strippers that have been murdered by some of their customers after work. This all goes with the hazard of the job. Some of them would do private parties and take their security with them. They would be pretty safe in general. There were some strippers who were mothers and went home to their family every night with a pocket full of ones.

What is the price of having people look at your body for money? What happens if you do marry someone that does not know you used to dance? Then they find out the hard way about your past? This has happened. Some people can accept it and others have broken up. What if your dad comes to the strip club with some of his buddies? He does not recognize you. He asks you for a lap dance because you look just like his wife when she was young. What if he does recognize you and has a heart attack? What if his buddies recognize you? Everyone has different answers to these serious scenarios. Stranger things have happened. Most dancers nowadays tell you up front how they make a living.

What if a mean group of children find out that your mother is a stripper? They are going to tease your child. This is what our society has come to. Where is the love in all this? The love is that God still loves all of us regardless of what mistakes we make. Love trumps sex every time, because God is love, and God trumps everything.

Letters of Love to the World from a Dark Man

Let us not forget the last part of the sexual revolution in the new century: porn sites. The most viewed sites on the Internet are pornography sites. This is big money. As we have progressed into the 21st century, virtual reality has taken control. AI is your new lover. People have developed virtual love programs. Many movies show hologram lovers that are exactly what you want. What do you really want? Do you really want love and attention from a computer? I guess it brings a new definition to safe sex.

What about touch? Can a computer touch you like a person? This brings a new meaning to computer love. Can a computer love you like a person? The answer is no. As we move forward into the future, we don't know what type of technology will be developed yet, but many people believe that people will have robot or android lovers. A machine without heart and soul. Would your android cheat on you? I guess not. But I will take real human love over a machine every day of the week. Love—how can you love a machine more than a person?

DRUGS

The purpose of my life has changed. We all change over time. There was a time in my life when I thought I would never stop using drugs. The mistakes I made as a young man are things of the past.

I quit drugs cold turkey. I quit fornication cold turkey. I quit alcohol cold turkey. I changed my whole life cold turkey.

Does God want us to do drugs? People want us to do drugs. Heroin, cocaine, and marijuana are the number-one exports of many countries, and big companies push them on us. The War on Drugs is a farce. Who has the money to send a submarine full of cocaine to America? What street-level dealer owns a private jet? Rich people and those connected to government. The government has not ended slavery—it has enhanced it. Drugs are a form of modern slavery.

Even prescription drugs can be addicting and sometimes unnecessary. Pain management clinics treat patients with legitimate severe pain, but some people go looking for a legal buzz. The opioid epidemic is a perfect example: opioids are highly controlled, yet overdoses are skyrocketing.

In hospitals, postoperative patients need opioids for pain control. Then they're sent home with Percocet, OxyContin, or fentanyl patches. Meanwhile, illicit users obtain these patches, melt them down, inject them—and sometimes die.

I want to revisit crack. It was society's downfall last century and remains prevalent today. Meth, ice, and fentanyl have emerged, but crack endures because a "hit" cost ten dollars. Dealers cut it with baking soda—hence the snap-crackle-pop effect—and often sold pure placebo. Laws had to adapt, creating charges like "intent to distribute placebo."

"Crack babies" were born to mothers using drugs during pregnancy. Many suffered low birth weight, brain damage, and failure to thrive. Yet some survived and thrived—proof of the resiliency of the human spirit and God's healing power.

People on prescription drugs are often worse off. Pharmaceutical companies push legal drugs more aggressively than any cartel. New life-saving drugs get tied up in research or bought out to protect profits. I experienced this in school when a promising discovery was shelved to avoid lawsuits. These practices happen constantly—saving lives is not always the priority. Companies and government work hand in hand to enrich the rich and keep the poor in place.

I take many medications: heart meds, diabetes drugs, blood-pressure pills, and kidney-disease treatments. Without them, I'd be sick or dead. Some skip meds because of side effects; I felt awful when I started mine, but I adapted. A friend died because he couldn't afford his prescriptions. We all would have paid for him, but he was too proud to ask. L-Train, we love you—may you rest in peace.

Life is convoluted, but we all need drugs of some kind: cold medicine, Benadryl, aspirin, Tylenol, Advil, weed, hops, tobacco, even Viagra. It's your choice; people need to help each other establish homeostasis.

An **addict** uses drugs daily—legal or illegal—not to get high but to function. They're thrown off when they miss a fix. I was one: I smoked weed all day; without it, people thought I was mad. I drank daily, mostly beer. Functional addicts exist—they work to support habit and family.

Letters of Love to the World from a Dark Man

An **abuser** lets drugs or alcohol control life. I knew a wealthy friend who called the dope man all day. He went to rehab, but only God changed his life; now he's drug-free, married, and happy.

A **user** uses drugs occasionally—partying or for a buzz. They don't keep drugs in their DNA and rarely buy more than they'll use.

A **tweak** chases uppers—crack, cocaine, meth. Tweaks flock to clubs and bathrooms in packs, wired until they crash.

A **dopey** favors downers—opioids or sedatives. Unmedicated, they become hyper; after a fix, they crash, craving ice cream to settle their stomach.

A **recreational user** is at the highest risk. They dabble and end up raped, injuring themselves or others—like driving after a laced joint and causing fatal accidents. If you don't do drugs, don't start. If you must, know the substance and your source.

Sick people need medication. I'm thankful for mine and for doctors, nurses, respiratory therapists, CNAs, pharmacists, and all healthcare workers. Caring for the sick is a ministry. Jesus healed the sick and raised the dead—and winebibbers remember he turned water into wine. God loves us all, regardless of how we cope with the world.

Letters of Love to the World from a Dark Man

VIOLENCE

Violence has occurred since the beginning of time. We come to the definition of violence: Ug busting an animal upside the head for survival. Ug busting Bug upside the head for trying to take his woman. Ug killing Bug for trying to take her again. All of these are acts of violence. Does the means justify the end? Of course it does. Let us take a brief tour through history.

In the beginning, God created man. Everything was good. Then Cain killed Abel.

That was violence in the first book of the Bible. Violence is all throughout the good book. In the beginning, man created violence. Man has a violent nature. Through violence, man is able to establish control over his society. Society is built on controlled violence. The military, police, and warriors are necessary. Governments can have no control without their enforcers. I pay tribute to all of the public servants—the police, the firemen, the EMS, and the military. They are dedicated to protecting the general population.

Man started off in a hunting and gathering society, living off the land, killing animals for their protein. People migrated throughout the world finding happy hunting grounds. Then man got too smart. He said, "I can stay on this land by the water and plant seeds and make things grow. This is my homeland." Homeland security—what a concept. As man began to call certain spaces his home, of course this caused discrepancies between groups of people. I think they call these conflicts war. War is a very specific type of violence, but again an unnecessary evil. Strong groups began to conquer other weaker groups. Many times, certain groups were either totally wiped out or absorbed by the more powerful group. Family, clan, tribes, nation.

The basis of society is the family. It takes violence to make a family. Someone has to be the enforcer. Without rules, children will run amok. I will mess a kid up. Take all of your bad kids and give them the business, because if they're not disciplined at home, they will end up getting disciplined by an outside enforcer. Punishments vary from family to family. Family values are passed down from generation to generation. Whenever you are lost for words, you think about the words that the person who raised you would say. All violence is control. If you do not control the child, you cannot control the adult. If the child lives long enough, one will be an adult longer than

Letters of Love to the World from a Dark Man

a child.

Back in the day, all of our parents would have been in jail if the laws were like they are now. They put child abuse charges on several different celebrities for disciplining their children. That's wrong. Better for the parents to discipline them than for them to be disciplined by society. I feel like people that discipline their children should be given an award. You cannot put every child in time out. Time out! What? We don't have any timeouts left. It's time for action.

Violence is a vicious cycle. One gang kills a member of another gang. Then they retaliate. The other gang blows up another gang member's house and kills his whole family. The rival gang then catches the other gang at a picnic on a Sunday in the park and kills a bunch of them, as well as a lot of innocent people. What is left of the last gang comes to avenge the death of their people and bombs the church where the families of the opposite gang go to church. Many people are at the church, but none of the gang members go to church. So their families are killed. Stop! Stop the violence. This is really how it goes down.

What are gangs? Gangs are groups of people that have a common ideology. They want to control and protect their area. Gangs range from loosely organized groups to entire nations—nations that are under one groove, indivisible, with liberty and justice for the few.

Friends go out to a party and dress alike and wear the same hairstyle. They are called a crew. They are all alike and like the same things and do not hang out with ugly girls. They are called a clique. People go through basic training and AIT and wear the same haircut, then you give them a gun and we call them Marines. A group of people who have a common heritage and religion, organized to make money and kill anyone who stands in their way, is called the mob. Mafia means "my family." An extensive amount of people joined together by common rule and set sovereign geographical boundaries is called a nation. There's a common thread here, as previously discussed. They all have an egocentric attitude: I am better than you and my way is the right way.

Let's break down the problem. My crew goes to a party having a good time dancing with women. One of my boys dances with another dude's girl—not just a dance, but a slow drag. Slow drag is a slow bump and grind. The problem with you grinding on her is that she is my girlfriend. He taps my buddy on the shoulder and says, "I'm cutting in." My buddy tells him, "Screw you!" Of course this escalates. They start to fight. "We got your

Letters of Love to the World from a Dark Man

back, brother." He and his crew assemble and the famous last words are spoken: "Let's take this outside!" We go outside and the scrap begins. It is 5 on 5, a fair fight. One guy is getting his butt whipped, and he runs to the trunk and gets his gun. He starts shooting. He kills one of my boys and one of their friends. He also kills an innocent bystander. Then after the funeral, we are all hurt. We promise to avenge his death. Of course, now starts the circle of violence.

The cheerleaders versus the other girls. Classic girl fights are more common among young women—hair being pulled, name-calling, internet fights. The worst one of all is "I got your boyfriend!" Here we go again. Two girls catch another girl from a rival clique alone. They start pushing her around. Passersby start to video the whole thing, and they beat the girl down. Her clothes come off, and they give her a black eye. Then they punch her in the stomach. Unknown to all parties involved, she was two months pregnant. She goes to the hospital and finds out that she was pregnant and loses her baby. She is devastated. She has to drop out of school to take counseling and contemplates the way to get back at the girls who caused the death of her baby.

She calls her boyfriend and tells him that she was pregnant. He is livid. He will not jump on a girl because he is the captain of the football team. The other girl's boyfriend is a nerd in the band. He corners him after band practice and beats him up and breaks his instrument. Now we have another gang war—the football team versus the band. The violence continues and grows until the principal calls a meeting between the groups. We all know how this ends up. After the meeting, it seems to be over. Until one day, one of the band members brings a gun to school in the instrument case. He shoots the captain of the football team, who was getting ready to graduate and had a full scholarship to Big State University. This happened all because some girls were texting nastygrams to each other and started all this other crazy stuff. Where does it end?

Or my family. The mafia is known for violence, but they're also known for loyalty. No need to discuss the mob history of violence. I kill one of yours, you kill two of mine. I travel to where you meet and I try to kill all of you. Anyone that survives comes back and tries to kill my whole family. And if I am alive, I'll go after all of your relatives. Where does it stop?

Nations are carved out of the blood of people. Blood, sweat, and tears is more than just a rock band. It is the way that this nation and all nations are forged. The mantra of the forefathers of this great nation was led by

Letters of Love to the World from a Dark Man

killing the indigenous people of this nation. Thank you to the many people who died pursuing "Manifest Destiny." The American population is now less than one percent indigenous people. This is called genocide. Genocide is large-scale homicide, justified. Many believe that if you want something, you take it—by hook or by crook.

The only problem is that now countries have nuclear weapons. I have a gun, you have a bigger gun. I have a bomb, you have a bigger bomb. My bomb is not as big as yours, but I can put it on a plane and kill some of your people. I can call my cousin in San Francisco and bomb the Golden Gate Bridge and kill some innocent people. This is called terrorism. Terrorism is stealth violence, like guerrilla warfare. I cannot beat you straight up, so I will attack you when you least expect it and kill whoever I can.

"My God, my God, why have you forsaken me?" These were the words of Jesus as he died for our sins—a violent death at the hands of the Romans. He was put to death by his own people. Yet Jesus did not retaliate. "Lord, they know not what they do." He rose from the dead and returned with even more love. Do we have the love to not retaliate? Love stops violence and heals us.

Charles Clark

WAR

What has been with us since the beginning of time? People—as well as animals—have fought over territory, a fight to the very end.

What is the difference between **war**, **fight**, **battle**, and **feud**?

War is a series of battles that decides a winner.

Fight is a one-time confrontation between opponents.

Battle is a large-scale confrontation between opponents.

Feud is a long-term confrontation that can stretch across generations.

Each term is largely defined by the *length* of the confrontation, yet the stakes change when there is loss of life or when an entire society is wiped out. Do we call that genocide? Domination? Annihilation? What do you call the death of an entire nation of people and their way of life? *America*? America—not just the United States. Our country, like so many others, was forged by war. War has plagued humankind throughout recorded history and long before it was ever documented. Is that bad? Perhaps not, if you happen to be on the winning side.

There are three kinds of war I struggle to understand: **civil**, **world**, and **holy**.

Civil War
There is nothing civil about war. The American Civil War was brutal and fought over resources, not slavery. The South resisted the high federal taxes on King Cotton. Before the war, Mississippi was the richest state in the Union; after Reconstruction it has remained one of the poorest.

World War
A world war suggests the entire planet is at war, yet some nations stayed neutral. Only the countries expecting a benefit—more resources—entered the conflict. Which is more valuable, life or resources? Resources, of course, as long as we are not the ones doing the fighting. Perhaps we should send the politicians—unarmed, hand-to-hand—to settle their disputes. Imagine two seventy-year-old men fighting to the death; wars might vanish overnight.

Charles Clark

Go to the Bible and you find **spiritual warfare**—a battle you cannot see, an eternal feud between good and evil. God, however, is eternal and perfect; He cannot be in conflict with Himself. Only flawed, finite humans wage spiritual war. War is ultimately a power struggle (see the chapter on Power). I would rather be powerful than rich. Money cannot always buy power, yet you can be both rich and powerful.

Consider Gandhi, Dr. Martin Luther King Jr., and Jesus: all died poor yet were spiritually rich. They fought and won the good fight—spiritual warfare played out on humanity's battlefield.

War involves death, and death leads to eternal life—life granted by God, the only eternal One. When we cannot reach a logical agreement, we fight, and afterward the stronger party takes what it wants. Occasionally the weaker side wins: David vs. Goliath, Moses vs. Rameses, Jesus vs. Rome. What is the common denominator? **God.**

David—a shepherd boy—defeated a champion soldier with one stone because God was on his side.

Moses led weaponless Hebrew slaves out of Egypt, overcoming the world's greatest power through God's might.

Letters of Love to the World from a Dark Man

Jesus eluded Roman soldiers as a child and later surrendered to crucifixion, yet triumphed over death itself.

God decides who wins and who loses every war. We rarely grasp His purposes, but His will prevails. At Calvary it looked like Rome and the Pharisees had triumphed. In truth, God won: Christ's resurrection opened heaven to us all. Humanity needed saving from itself, not from God.

Before humans, plants and animals existed without sin. Sin arrived with free-willed humanity. People wage war on animals and ultimately conquer them, yet even the fiercest storms remind us we can never conquer God.

War is simple: **loss of life is loss of love, loss of love is loss of God, and loss of God is death.**

A mother cries when her son dies
A child can't understand why it won't see Daddy again
A wife feels alone when her husband is dead and gone
Everyone loses in war—need I say more?

DEATH

Recently, I have been going to a lot of funerals. I see death every day as a nurse. This is hard. I do not react to it like I used to. I've grown somewhat immune to it. I guess that one day I will succumb to it also. Everyone wants to get to heaven, but nobody wants to die. When we speak of death, we are speaking of a physical death, not a spiritual death. We mourn, we cry, but why? Should we not rejoice for a person getting eternal life? Never dying, perfect peace.

One of my best friends died. We were in first grade together. I thought that we would be young forever. Only God is forever. Death is imminent for man. As soon as you're born, you start to die. Death is like a period at the end of the sentence. It is a small thing, but it is something big. Look at life. What is life but a timeline? Death is the end of that timeline for that individual, but time goes on for everyone else.

They recently said that the universe was 13.5 billion years old. What if you added 13.5 billion to 13.5 billion? That would equal 27 billion. Twenty-seven billion does not equal eternity or infinity. God is infinite. Time is infinite. These measures of time are for man, not God. Time before time, and time after time.

Death is the ultimate sacrifice. Once you are dead, all of your pain and struggles go away. Hunger, thirst, all subside. Your needs as a biosphere and the demands of the universe are all gone. As a matter of fact, that dynamic interaction between our organism and its surroundings ceases to exist. Life is a constant competition of an organism struggling to survive in a plenum. Resources are scarce with many competitors. We either move or die.

The process of dying can be quick. We can be overcome by diseases that lead to morbidity. Slow sickness can lead to death, but many times sickness can lead to victory—battling an infirmity to overcome cancer. People survive to rehab from a severe car accident. That is incredible. Living beyond a childhood illness shows the strength of the human spirit. Children never give up and never let go. They fight, fight, fight and never give up.

We find many people who say, "Do I have anything to live for?" Why do people attempt suicide? You are going to die anyway. Take your time—literally take your time. Don't throw it away. The time you have here is limited and precious.

Therefore, living life—how should you live your life? Cautious? Wild? How? There's no right answer. Everything is contingent on who you are. You are born to be you. Once again, I pose the question: How do you live your life? You live your life according to what you are willing to die for. Family, honor, love, and God are all things worth living for. God is the ultimate honor.

To honor is to pray. When we pray, we are saying that there is something or someone greater than ourselves. Otherwise, we are talking to ourselves for nothing. We are talking to ourselves. When we die, we have nowhere to go. To hell is the same as going nowhere—that our spiritual lives are not real. God is not real. God is real. But some people say that certain people die for nothing. That is the reality and that is their epitaph. Oh well, I live for something greater. Something I am willing to die for.

A true believer is willing to die for what they believe in. The operative word is "in." Prepositions are usually very small words with big meanings. In, out, under, above, and below are commonly used words in sentences. We meet our maker, and if we are under the blood of Jesus Christ, we have a gift that no one could possibly give us but God. The gift of eternal life. Our death becomes life because of the death of Jesus. We die and are buried. We will be judged at the end of that. We could never be judged. God knows what really happens.

We all have religious explanations, but what do we see? For all things, the spirit never dies. The Holy Spirit is with us at all times. If the Holy Spirit is immune to death, then we can never die. All organisms are born to die. God created us all. We are for the glorification of God. God has created a dynamic system that is flawless. Man tries to control God's creation by building buildings, building roads, and other alterations to God's creation. Man has found no way to defeat death. Death is God's ultimate trump card. Regardless of how long you live, you will never outlive God. Just lay down and die.

We are convicted to do the work of God—that is why we were born. We are put here to do what he wants us to do, regardless of what we think. That is our purpose. We must find out our purpose. Do you know your purpose? All of us make mistakes. Some of us make more mistakes than others but still come out being a blessing to the world. When children are stillborn, what is God's purpose? Why do we constantly question the will of God? Why do some people live to be over 100 years old? Only God knows.

I do not have all the answers, but God convicted me to

write this book. This is my gift to the world. I worked on this book for over 30 years. One day God told me to finish it. The drive and the time it takes to write a book is unreal. Is God calling? I do not know, but what I do know is that we are all here for a special purpose. The purpose that God has set forth for us is sometimes different than our own individual aspirations. In order to be successful in life, God's plan and man's plan have to be congruent, because God is still in charge.

What if someone had a gun to your head—will you renounce God? Or will you tell them to go ahead and shoot? "Praise the Devil and I will let you live." What would you say? Regardless of what your choice is, you're going to die. Death is the ultimate sacrifice. I would not renounce my savior. Jesus made the ultimate sacrifice so that we could have an eternal home. Jesus said we are saved by faith. Faith without works is dead. Pull the trigger because I'm going straight to heaven. You may shoot me because I'm going to die anyway. I'd rather die loving the Lord.

There are different religions, but only one God. Some people think that listening to orchestra music forever would be heavenly. Other people believe that listening to that same music would be hell. The definition of heaven and hell are personal for each individual. Death is a sacrifice. A sacrifice to get to the next level—a true field of dreams. Our lives are not defined by the way we live, but by the way we die.

Would you take a bullet for a loved one? Could you jump into a body of water not knowing how to swim and try to save a stranger? Could you sacrifice your own life for the greater good of society? Do you think that you could truly give your life for what you believe in? These are questions that you must ask yourself. What are you willing to die for? That may be your purpose in life. To be able to stand for something and die for it. That is true greatness.

God chose his son to die for our souls. God chose other great leaders to die for their people. Abraham was willing to sacrifice his son to God. It was blind obedience. He did not question God. In a battle, a soldier dives on a land mine to save his troop. People devote their entire lives to one cause, one formula, one thing—a commitment to the greater good.

What is your purpose? I adjure every person in the world to discover themselves and find their purpose. Be the light before you see the light.

RELIGION

Oh! One of the toughest subjects in the world. The things that people have gone to war for. First, let us explore what religion is and what religion is not. God created man. Man, then in turn, created God! God does not need man, but man does need God to explain his existence.

Religion is man trying to explain his existence. We go through life trying to answer the question: Why am I here? We continually go on retreat to the mountains, trying to find ourselves. Constantly trying to get closer to God. God is right here! We go through life looking for God, and he is always by our side. God is always with you.

In the beginning, God created who? Man! A man with the IQ of 40. There was no written language, no education, no books. What do you think? Where was Jesus? Where was Moses? Nowhere to be found. God was there. He said, "I have no name. I am who I am." Man, even at the early stages of his development, worshiped God. God to him was the sun, the moon, or possibly himself. Man was made in the image of God. In the world of the universal aura, God is equal to the entropy of the universe. God is all that is! You, your enemy, your garbage—they are all part of God. God is everything. You and everyone else that is alive and living are in a plenum. Okay, boys and girls, go get your dictionaries and philosophy books. The last paragraph was a monster on religion.

I'm leaving. I grew up Catholic. I've been Catholic all my life. I've been to all kinds of churches. I've been to temple. I've prayed with people from different religions. Some of the best people I know are religions other than Christianity. Some of the dirtiest people I know are Christians. Why do I bring out this point? This is because of all religions, Christians judge people more than any other religion. They tell you that if you're not a Christian, you're going to hell. Where in the hell are you going? You are not going to—you cannot judge me. We are all part of God. We are all human.

Christians tell me that because I'm Catholic, I need to be saved. Who are you, a lifeguard? Save yourself! Save by your own faith. Faith is blind—you believe in something or someone you cannot see, but what you can feel. What you feel is real.

Therefore, point by point, let me enumerate the important points of this chapter. I refuse to educate you as you read.

You need to raise yourself. Words you do not know—find the definition for yourself. People have said that religion is the opiate of the masses. The Roman Empire changed from pagan to Catholic. That is how Roman Catholic came about. This was a funny transition from Roman mythology to Christianity at that time. Why? Because the Roman Catholic religion makes slaves more passive.

Christianity is a beautiful, loving, humanistic religion. A religion based on the fact that God became man. Christianity is one of the only religions in the world where God became man and actually took human form. Many religions have said that the gods came down from heaven and had children with humans, but Jesus Christ is the only one that actually came down from heaven and was born as man.

Egyptians believed in Ra, Horus, and the holy mother Isis. Ra was the god of the sun, equivalent to God the Father. Horus was equivalent to the Holy Spirit, supposedly the equivalent to Jesus Christ, and of course Isis was equivalent to the Virgin Mary. This was the Holy Trinity, even prior to Christianity having a Holy Trinity. How interesting. Jews were held in captivity by Egyptians for 400 years. Some people say that they adopted these ideologies from their captors.

Jews wrote the Torah. The Torah is what most Christians call the Old Testament, but actually the Torah is the first five chapters of the Old Testament. The Old Testament is the first half of the Bible. The Old Testament describes the trials and tribulations of the Jewish people. The Old Testament concentrates on God the Father. It shows that God was trying to lead the people in a certain direction, but they were not willing to follow the directions he gave. God was a god of great power in the Old Testament. He brought wrath, plagues, and death to all who challenged him! God the Father is a god of power and might, the god of vengeance and war. The God that would annihilate your enemy. God the Father is the true and living God.

Let us transcend back to the god of the bushman. It is said that man was first created in Africa—this is what research shows. The basis of most African religions is the family. It is very important to know your family, ancestry, and history. That is also true for many Eastern religions. They believe that when you do something to disgrace yourself, you disgrace all of your ancestors—not just your mother and father, but all of them. We are all the summation of all our ancestors. This spilled over to the creation of tribes. Tribes turned into clans. Clans turned into nations.

"In God We Trust"—that is not only something on our money, but that is something that everyone should believe. Different religions think different things. Many religions think that my God is better than yours. My God can beat your God. My God is bigger than your God, and not because I just capitalize it. The God of the bushman was simple and complete. I am God, yet I love and think that there is something greater than me. I love it and I respect it, but I don't know what it is.

As man has migrated and spread to all the ends of the Earth, he has physically changed and adapted to be conducive to his environment. These differences, he has personalized—religion and customs. Therefore, God has been personalized. The strongest people always conquer weaker people and turn them to their religion and customs. The bushman is still in the bush today, doing what he did 1 million years ago. Is he right or is he wrong? Is it so bad to be living the same way that his prehistoric ancestors lived? What is prehistoric? There's no such thing. "Pre" means before. There is no time before time, except for God. Therefore, the history of these people was passed on by mouth, not written down because they had no written language.

Truth and love are things relative to moral reality. Religion gives you morals. Morals are different for every religion and society. In Eastern religions, some suicides are considered to be a death with honor. In other religions,

Letters of Love to the World from a Dark Man

it is honorable to kill your enemy and yourself at the same time, like a suicide bomber, and you will go straight to heaven. Kamikaze bombers used in World War II were used to attack enemy ships, and yet the pilots of the planes knew that they would die, but as long as they killed some of the enemies, they were going straight to heaven.

Religion has been at the crux of war since the Crusades. Look at the slave trade—people went into the jungle with the Bible in one hand and a sword in the other. All of the ancestors of Africans are now Christians. They were terrorized and converted to a religion that was not theirs. Now their progeny embraces the religion that enslaved them and took all of their land and resources. Religion has spread more by war than anything else.

When Spain was invaded during the Crusades, it was occupied for almost 400 years. This led to the spread of Islam. The conquistadors invaded Mexico and fought the Aztecs and killed them by disease. They gave them their religion and language. South America is one of the strongholds of not only Catholicism but also Spanish.

For me, I am a savage. Savages were holding back the settlers from Manifest Destiny. It is the will of God that the United States of America go from sea to shining sea.

The indigenous people were brutally murdered by the poor settlers. Did God say that it was okay? According to some people, they would say it is the will of God! God said no such thing.

The religions of the indigenous people were based on the principles of peace and love. Love of the land, love of God, and that the land belonged to no one because it was God's. That we are all part of one big soul. That religion said that you must love the land and animals and only take what you need. The bison was the phenomenal mainstay of the indigenous people of the plains. The civilized people realized that if you kill the mainstay of these people, you also kill them. Kill a buffalo, kill an indigenous person. What does it matter? Both of them are animals. Animals like the slaves that were born in this country—they were not even counted in the Constitution of the United States until the 3/5 Amendment came about for tax purposes. Yet the slaves were only property, not people. That was being a good Christian.

Did God tell the wasps to kill the indigenous people and enslave the slaves? Sure did! The Bible tells you to multiply and take dominion over the Earth. When the slaves were converted to Christianity during slavery, did God save them from being raped, whipped, murdered, or worked to death? Sure did. At the end of your life, you will have a greater gift—to go to heaven. Heaven is your reward. The slaves had to go straight to heaven because their life was a living hell.

If my master and I are praying to the same God, then heaven has to be segregated too. Because if we go to the same heaven together, I'm going to whip him when I see him up there. I have the whip now! What happens if you see your enemies in heaven? Are you going to fight in heaven? What is heaven? Is it a place beyond the clouds? We fly in the clouds all the time. Heaven is not hidden in the clouds. It's not hiding up there with all of the saints and my great-grandparents.

All religions have someplace of peace and rest. A place where, regardless of how good or bad your life was, there is an eternal resting place of peace and solace. What happens to people when they change religions? Some people are born Christian and convert to Islam or Buddhism. Does God change? No! God cannot change. God is constant and infinite. I have a new religion, and it is to choose God.

Man has finite knowledge and can only think of God in simple terms. We must realize that God does not change, but man changes, and that sometimes you have to change directions to find a pathway to the same place. God is a universal constant. God is not a little old man sitting on a throne. God is not the man at the end of the rainbow, as in some movie. God is not a man at all! God is a spirit. A spirit has no parts. A spirit has no sexuality.

Man chooses a way for him to better understand God. Understanding yourself is the key to understanding God. Know yourself and God is there. Developing the relationship between God and self is the apex of being alive. Religion is for man, not God. God does not care how you worship him. He cares how you love yourself and love others.

People have used religion to separate people since the beginning of time. People should have respect for other people's religion. People should settle their differences in a godly manner. God wants us all to be united. We are all God's children. God is love.

THE BIBLE

The Bible is called the good book. The Bible is the largest-selling book in the world. It is always number one on the bestsellers list. Let us take a look at the Bible. The Old Testament itself is a history of the Hebrews—God's chosen people. What is meant by God's chosen people? The same people he chose are the same ones that put Jesus Christ to death. The same people that do not necessarily believe in the New Testament. The same people who believe that the savior is still coming. Do you believe in the Torah? The Torah is simply the first five books of the Old Testament. They were written by Moses. The Bible combines the Old and New Testament. It is a chronicle of Israeli people and the life of Christ.

We need to explore the common theme here. The Bible is a book of life. In the beginning, the Hebrews were a nomadic people that lived in poverty and were enslaved by the Egyptians. They were dominated by the Roman Empire. Both empires not only dominated the Hebrew people but influenced their culture. Creation was explained by a man 3,000 years ago. What is the explanation of modern man? Was the world created in seven days? Yes, seven days in God's time. Man can only think in finite terms.

The story of Evolution and Genesis are totally supported by science. Science and religion both explain creation. Day one, let there be light. Was this the Big Bang? Day two, God created the heavens and the earth. Which Big Bang was this? Some people say that the universe has exploded; others say that it may implode. How can one explain that each planet has a spin and an orbit? The mass called the Sun and the stars are fixed units of light. They are heat and energy. Why don't they move? Why does our solar system and a molecule have the same structure? The nucleus is fixed and the electrons travel around the heat. The Sun is the nucleus of our solar system and the planets orbit around it. Of course, we have shooting stars, comets, and galactic storms. Man cannot throw a baseball and make it spin in the same place for 12 billion years. "Let there be light" displays the infinite power of God. It is shown in the positioning of the planets.

The mass called Earth is perfectly positioned from the Sun to support life. When the land was formed, it was one parcel of land. After many years, the Continental Divide occurred. The separation of land and water took years. A day to God, billions of years of time to man. The creation

Letters of Love to the World from a Dark Man

of the planets and vegetation took one day for God, but for man it was billions of years. Day four, God created animals. He created different species of animals. It took millions of years to create all the different species. The evolution of animals took years. What about the thought that man evolved from apes? If that was true, then why don't apes keep turning into people? God created man as a separate and special being that God created last. Day seven, he rested. God lets man do anything he pleases. God is a free will God. God gave man dominion over the Earth and man has taken the world in the direction that he wants. God gives man freedom of choice. Choice and freedom are the keys to creation.

Man now has taken over creation. No, man has not created anything that God does not allow. God has not created monsters, vampires, or werewolves. Man came up with those ridiculous creatures. God created things of beauty and love.

Let us push forward in the book. We go to the story of Adam and Eve. They lived in the Garden of Eden. The Garden of Eden was probably in the Mesopotamian River Valley. Science says that the oldest bones of man were found in Tanzania. This is a story of good and evil. The dichotomy between good and evil are the choices of man. Man has the power to make a choice. The choice was a difficult choice. Good or evil exist according to the morals of its society. At that time in history, many people worshiped snakes. They were considered powerful and masterful, even as a sign of sexual fertility. Trees and bushes were also symbols of fertility and good. This is a story of God setting the rules that man should obey. God said, "Place no other God before me." God is a jealous God. God is God. God is good.

The Bible is written by man, not God. God sent people visions. God sent me visions to write this book. The Bible is a book. Whether you like it or not, the Bible is a history book. It shows the struggles of the Hebrew people. They have been fighting for land since the beginning of time. The land that they seek is the Gaza Strip and Israel proper. I'm happy to see that the nomadic people finally have a place to settle. Israel is backed by the United States; therefore, might makes right.

The Bible is also a book of laws. The Ten Commandments are the basic laws of the Jewish people. The Christians not only adopted these laws but used the life of Christ as a template for how they should lead a godly life. The difference between the Jews and the Christians is that Christians believe Jesus is the son of God and the Jews believe that the Messiah is still coming.

Letters of Love to the World from a Dark Man

Let us look at the life of Christ. He was born homeless—no medical benefits, no welfare, no food stamps. He was born in a barn. What a hard life. He was born a poor, innocent child. A child! He and the Holy Family had to flee to Egypt to get away from the Romans. He lived there for several years. Then he shows back up at about the age of 12. He was speaking at the temple when he was 12 years old. Then he disappeared again for 20 years. There are no gospels or writings of the life of Jesus for 20 years. What did he do for 20 years? He learned to be a carpenter. He is a modern-day construction worker—working in the dirt, doing manual labor.

Jesus then started to recruit his apostles. He chose them one by one. All different. Paul was the rich one. All of the rest of them were poor men. Jesus was homeless most of his life. You don't see anywhere in the Bible where he had a home, even though he was a carpenter and was probably able to build a house here on earth. He said that he was building his mansion in heaven.

If Jesus were alive today, they would say that Jesus hung around with the pimps, the pushers, the drug addicts, the alcoholics, and prostitutes. He hung out with the street people of today. The religious leaders admonished him. These were the Pharisees and the Sadducees—the very same people that would be good Christians today. These are the same people who found any reason that they could think of to have Christ put to death.

Jesus went to the temple and he started tearing stuff up. He got rid of the tainted doves. Jesus hardly ever got upset, except at the temple. I see the same parallel life that he saw back then at the temple. People going to church all dressed up and looking down on other people that do not have as much as them. Churches taking direct deposit out of the parishioners' checking accounts. Jesus did not ever take money. Jesus did not collect tithes. Jesus did not have a horse or a camel. He was always walking and living off the fat of the land.

There are too many TV evangelists that are making millions of dollars. They are driving big fancy cars. They live a life of luxury. I hate that. Do reverends give back to their patrons when they collect too much money? No. I have never seen a church with a rebate program. They keep it in their pockets. The clergy is responsible to answer to God. The pastor is supposed to look good. He is supposed to be dressed well. If a member of the clergy is not dapper, does that mean that they are not a godly person? There are some preachers and pastors who don't have large congregations and don't make a lot of money. They are truly called by God. Even some of the rich ones are called by God. People need to know that there's a difference between God calling you and you becoming a reverend for all the wrong reasons.

"It is as difficult for a rich man to get into heaven as it is for a camel to go through the eye of a needle." God does not like ugly and not so much for pretty either. Speaking of the eye of the needle, it was a tax gate in between the provinces. It was the smallest one, usually for children. The Romans charged a toll for going from one province to the other.

Any preacher, bishop, pope, reverend, deacon, or religious leader is responsible for leading the flock in the right direction. No one can save your soul but you. You and only you! You will die by yourself. The choir will not die with you. You and God are one. You are a part of God. Jesus lives with you. The Holy Spirit is the forgotten and misunderstood part of the Holy Trinity. The Holy Spirit lives in everyone and everything—even evil people. You may be good to someone else, and vice versa. In the Middle East, they have monuments about different wars—monuments that could represent something negative in the United States.

There have been many religious leaders who all died poor: Jesus, Dr. Martin Luther King, Malcolm X, and Gandhi. They all died poor and would not accept riches for souls.

Some religious leaders start off poor, then sell their souls for fame and fortune. They start off on a mission to save souls, then become rich. Some may have helicopters, airplanes, and multiple cars. Yet the death of many great leaders is directed by God. When you die for what you believe in, the people after you believe in you and you become entrenched in the heart of man.

Many people have the job of supporting the church. The church does not mean the building—the people are the church. Back to the life of Jesus: there were two important women in his life. Mary Magdalene and his mother Mary. These two ladies were totally different. One was a virgin, and the other was a prostitute. How much greater of a dichotomy can you have? The story of these two ladies gives us examples of how women should act. Jesus' mother was a holy woman, good, and supported her son. She loved him. Mary Magdalene was the opposite. But when she met Jesus, she changed her life. She didn't work the streets anymore. She went with Jesus and the apostles to all the different regions. She was an example that we can all change our lives—that we can all be better than we were. That each day is a new day to re-create ourselves. That is the challenge before us.

The greatest love of all is the love of God. Jesus was a perfect example of how a man should love his family.

Letters of Love to the World from a Dark Man

Jesus loved his apostles. They were his friends as well as his family. He loved his mother and everybody he touched.

The books of Judges and Kings describe the lives of David and Solomon and their children. Children are life. God's greatest gift to each and every one of us is the gift of life. The ability to create life is God's gift to man. He gave man the gift of being able to create in his own image. Your children look like you because God gave you the opportunity to procreate. The people in the Old Testament that followed God's will were blessed. Solomon was cursed when he disobeyed God. David was cursed when he disobeyed God's will. God does not care what people think. God is not nice. God will strike you down and send you to hell. God in the Old Testament is a God of power and might—one that does not play. One that kills whole armies, newborns, enemies, and those that disobey his will. "Thy will be done, not my will be done."

God of the New Testament was a merciful God. Jesus' first miracle was turning water into wine. The wine bibbers always remember that. Sounds like Jesus was having a good time. God never says that we cannot enjoy our life. There's nowhere in the Bible where it says that you cannot drink alcohol. It says not to be a drunk. In other words, God's law is man's law—don't get a DUI. Many people say that Jesus' wine was nonalcoholic, that it was juice. The Bible said he made wine, not juice. He could've made gasoline out of water. Jesus is God. He can make whatever he wants.

People take the Bible and add and subtract from it as they see fit. There are books missing from the Bible. Certain translations have more books than others. The Bible is a book that has been translated from one language to another. There are always things that are lost in translation from one language to another because of idiomatic phrases. Certain things said in one language can only be said in that language. Every time something is translated, it changes its meaning. The theologians that translated the Bible were mostly monks. There are no Jewish monks or Baptist monks.

The truth is the light. The people of "The Way" were the original beacon of Christianity. Outsiders called them this because of the way that they treated each other. The Church was later called the Catholic Church prior to the Protestant Reformation. We all know that the Church at that time may have needed some changes, but this chapter is about the Bible. The Bible was written by all men. The Bible was written in Greek, Hebrew, and Aramaic, then translated into Latin, German, and English, then every other language.

The Bible is a book of instructions. If you follow instructions, you get good outcomes. If you do not follow the instructions, things don't go so well. It is a written record of what has happened. The main problem with most people is that they cannot follow instructions. People always try to put something together without reading the directions. God gives you specific directions. The Bible is a book of directions for your life. Read the label carefully! Follow the directions!

The precepts of society are about freedom. Freedom means you do not have to follow directions. Even though God gives us free will, human nature inherently wants to do anything. Therefore, we get into an ethical crossfire. Is man inherently good or bad? What the world has shown us is that man is inherently bad—bad to the bone. Man has killed man all throughout the Bible. Cain killed Abel. The Romans killed Jews. Jews killed Jesus.

God is love. The Bible shows us that love conquers all evil. Love is the ultimate weapon against everything. God is love. If there is one power I wish I had, it would be the power of love.

Charles Clark

GOD

The key is that God is on the throne. Many things that I've already written in this book have come to pass. I am a messenger of God. God is at the center of our lives whether we believe it or not. God is in it. God is so much more than our exceedingly small brains can comprehend—beyond our religion and belief. The Holy Spirit is our part of God. The Holy Spirit is in all of us. Other religions talk about one big soul. This is very true. We are all one.

How could heaven exist as man exists on earth? Is heaven integrated or segregated? Are certain people over here and certain people over there? Is there a dividing line between different types of people in heaven?

No! Does God talk to us in our native language? How did God learn all of these languages? God has infinite understanding of all the languages we speak. We are all the same color—all the same to God. God is the meaning of life. God is a breath of fresh air.

Letters of Love to the World from a Dark Man

God wants us to be ourselves, even if that is being a villain. Without villains, there are no heroes. Heroes are created by adversity and despair. Villains cause despair. Look at the story of Moses and Rameses. Both are in history. God freed the Jewish slaves from Rameses. Rameses was a villain to the Jews. After Exodus, the Jews left Egypt. Rameses was a hero in his country and he lived for many more years until the age of almost 90 years old. You may be a hero to the Egyptians.

Science and history are truly remarkable according to who is writing the story. The truth can be slanted in either direction depending on who is writing the story. Take the story of the Cowboys and the Indians. The Jews and the Gentiles. Where am I going with this? God loves all of us. There is a degree of selfishness that people show in times of war. Many people are slaughtered. The children on both sides lose. When can we start to live by this and realize the fact that God is for everyone? God is for the sinners and the saved. God's chosen people are those that believe in him. Groups of people have experienced slavery and mass genocide throughout history.

Family is the main thing that is missing from our society today. The family is the main thing that allows people from other countries to come to America. Is God only for certain people? God is for everyone. You have to choose

God. People have used religion throughout the ages to separate people, not to unify them.

Why do people turn away from religion? Apostasy is a disease. People have travail and pain occur in their lives and they blame God. This causes them to question their beliefs. Therefore, they lose faith and worry about what they lost instead of thanking God for what they have.

How can God bring people together? God tries to bring people together, but people always look at their differences. Many people have sold their souls to the devil. People are making lots of money. Many people are billionaires and millionaires. There are over 2,200 billionaires and over 16,000,000 millionaires in the world. The 10 richest people in the world have over half the wealth in the entire world. These are people who are icons. People look up to these people because they have done extremely well financially. They need to give back to the people. Also, God has blessed them with wealth and prosperity. Prosperity comes with responsibility.

When you are successful, you are a role model. People in this country associate success with money. No one is born into royalty here. Royalty comes with money in the United States. "In God We Trust" is on our money. They forgot the part about "All Others Pay." Some people have enough sense to realize that the responsibility to the community is great.

This country has always been the biggest thug on our planet. This country and every nation shall be judged by God for their wrongdoing and atrocities. The final destination of every nation is left up to God. Do you think that you won't be judged by God? You will. You'll be judged by your actions, not your thoughts. Actions speak louder than words.

God is "DOG" spelled backwards. Dog is supposed to be man's best friend, but as we all know, God is truly man's best friend. God does all of the things a dog does—is watching over you. God cares for you and loves you like a dog, unconditionally. When you come home from work and you had a bad day, God is right there by your side.

Some people think that God is going to get you. I've heard that so many times in my life. It is ridiculous. I honestly believe that God will get you one way or the other. We are all interconnected. Whatever you do comes back to you. How can you get away if God is ubiquitous? There's nowhere you can hide from God.

People have used God to control people for years. Some say that religion is the opiate of the masses. I say that the masses are like sheep. People have the proclivity to follow other people because when something goes wrong, they can just blame it on their leader. People blame God for their mistakes. They blame the devil. They blame everyone else but themselves. People don't want to own up to their own failures. They are always ready to take credit for their success, but blame everyone else for their misfortunes.

God is my dog. He watches me, he protects me. God is my best friend. God will judge all of us. We will all be judged by the same God. We all have the same needs. We speak different languages, different religions, different cultures, and different parts of the world. In this country you might be born Catholic, Baptist, or Jewish. If you change religions, did you change God? No, of course not. This person changed channels.

God comes to you through your senses. You have to feel God to believe in God. People feel the spirit in church. People are moved when they hear a certain song. Other people go to a place in their house that they consider a prayer room. Many people feel one with nature. We all have a certain sense of solitude and spirituality at some times in our lives. Where do we get this warm and fuzzy feeling from?

Letters of Love to the World from a Dark Man

People who are atheists say God does not exist. They believe that the universe is self-determined. They are right—God is self-determined. God is all that exists. God is the potential energy of the entire universe. A religious point of view seems like a scientific explanation. God is the simplest thing that we take for granted: no breath, no life, no God.

The reason that I have gone into this so extensively is because God is the center of my life. God is the center of all our lives, whether we believe it or not! I've gone through a lot in my life. What is your relationship with God? On judgment day, there will be no mommy or daddy. No one will die with you. You will be on your own—no church members and other medians.

Ancient religions believed that God was in the sky. They believed that God actively took part in the everyday lives of humans. Some people believed that God is nature. There was no need to look any further than nature itself. People should realize that God does not come from outside. God is within you. God is right there in your life. In your entire life, you live your life with God. A person develops a personal relationship with God.

Everyone can be great, even if it is being great at mediocrity. Choice is a key to freedom in life. Life is full of choices. God knows what we're going to do, but he allows us the freedom to live our lives. Without freedom, we can revisit the theory of predestination and existentialism, stating that man has no freedom or control over life. God lives with each of us. God gives us life and we take the ball and run with it.

Life is a circle. As soon as you're born, you start to die. It is inevitable. Death is guaranteed. Life after death is guaranteed. People talk about near-death experiences and seeing. People described the same thing. They all talked about seeing a light. They felt that if they reached the light, they would've crossed over. Your job in life is to be light before you see the light.

Therefore, heaven, hell, and the afterlife are metaphysical—beyond the physical realm, beyond the mental realm, but a true spiritual realm. The spirit is boundless. The spirit is the part of us that God gives us. We are all parts of God. We do not treat each other like we are one. People have a selfish nature. Everything is about me. Me first, and other people get the leftovers. God's chosen people, God's country, God made us first, we have God's grace—all of these phrases are true. God loves everybody.

Letters of Love to the World from a Dark Man

GOD is GOOD

If you take the GOD out of GOOD, you have O left.

GOOD - GOD = O

This is another mathematical explanation for GOD.

Charles Clark

THE MESSAGE

Does God not need us? I guess he does—God created us. We need God. Why is man the only creature that worships God? Why is man the only creature that wants to play God?

Animals do not have religion. Animals do not seek eternal truth; animals do not seek eternal life. Are animals in the image of God? There goes that word "image." Animals and plants go about their lives doing exactly what God created them to do. They accomplish their purpose. Predators hunt prey. Scavengers clean up. Animals of prey are an integral part of the food chain. Plants supply food and oxygen, as well as stabilize the soil. God created a perfect ecosystem.

Man has done everything he can to destroy it. Pollution is all over the planet. Strip mining has destroyed the earth. Global warming is changing the climate. As we deforest the land, the animals don't have anywhere to live, and you wonder why bears and wolves are in your backyard. Many animals are extinct because people kill animals for

Letters of Love to the World from a Dark Man

sport. The list goes on and on, to show how our society has changed the face of the earth. This change is what we call progress.

Let's tie up all the loose ends. What is the message of this book? We have been on a long, arduous journey. The message is that God wants you to love everyone and everything, because God is everything. People have hated each other since the beginning of time. People are different, but yet we are all the same. The chapter on racism shows why God does not want people to be racist. Love people different from you. People should not be prejudiced.

Some of my best friends had never been around people of a different race before. As it turned out, I turned out to be their brother. I love everyone. Just because we are different, it does not mean that we can't be friends. If you see a spotted elephant, it doesn't mean that the elephant has chicken pox.

God wants us to have sex. Sex is not bad. Sex is for procreation between two people that are married and love each other. Having sex just for fun is not why we were made sexual beings. The moral judgment of this book does not downplay or judge anyone's lifestyle. I have had sex many, many times. Sex and love are two different things. You can love someone without having sex with them, and you can have sex with someone and not even know their name. Sex is probably the root of my greatest sins. I cannot judge anyone!

Sex is how most of us got here, besides test tube babies. Without sex there will be no people or anything else. All creatures—plants, microbes, and animals—have some type of reproductive process. You have a one-night stand and out comes a baby. Did the baby commit a sin? No. Did the baby have a choice in the matter? No. The child is a child of God. God can take the bad and make something good out of it.

God does not want us to be violent. Violence is bad. Violence perpetuates more violence. Cain killed Abel. Are you to be Abel? "Can" means do you have the ability to do something. Are you able to love, or can you not? Who are you—Cain or Abel? Are you able, or can? This book takes words and numbers and picks them apart and tries to explain them in a different light! So many people have lived their lives in darkness that the light hurts their eyes. God is the light of the world.

God wants us to read the Bible—not just read the Bible, but to live by the Bible. Can you live by the Bible? Can you live a truly godly life? It is harder than it seems. How can a preacher be racist? If you're racist, where are you leading your flock? Are you setting a good example? Don't you love everyone? If you are not, then you are leading the flock astray. In most cases, Sunday is the most segregated day of the week. There are some churches that have a mixture of different nationalities, but for the most part, most churches have a homogenous pool of one nationality of people.

People should follow God. Do not follow man. Man will lead you astray every time. Believe in God. God will never fail you. God is forever. Man will die. Believe in the everlasting God who wants us to have money. The chapter on money expands on the fact that it is as hard for a camel to pass through the eye of a needle as it is for a rich man to get into heaven. This is something that theologians have argued about for centuries. "The eye of a needle" was a gate in the holy land that was set up for children to pass through to collect taxes by the Romans. Some people say that it refers to a sewing needle. I leave your decision up to you.

Do not let money change you or rule your life. Make money. Don't let money make you. What about the saying, "Money is the root of all evil"? This is true if you worship money—if you are not worshiping God. God is a jealous God. Money is a necessary evil in today's world.

Charles Clark

If you cannot afford this book, you need to go get some more money. It costs money to print this book and also takes the ability to read, which means you are educated and you have the necessary funds to buy this book.

God does not want us to go to war. A prayer war is acceptable—be a prayer warrior. Pray for good. Pray to fight injustice, racism, evil, prejudice, ignorance, disease, and poverty. We have to fight every day to make this world a better place. A place to raise our children. A place to leave our grandchildren and great-grandchildren, and generations to come. This is their world. A gift passed on from generation to generation.

The Earth is our responsibility. We have to take care of it. God handed it over to us and he gave us a paradise. What have we turned the world into? Some people say that the world is a living hell, while other people live in the lap of luxury, like heaven on earth. There can be no rich people without poor people. Be rich in spirit, be kind and thoughtful. Be benevolent to people. Feel the love.

I feel love.

CONCLUSION

How do you edit a book that you've worked on for most of your life? I started this book in my 30s, or maybe my late 20s. It all runs together now.

It fascinates me how well I remember my entire life—even being a baby. I do not remember coming out of the womb, but I can think back to being maybe one or two years old. When my dad used to come home from work, I would get so excited and I would jump up and down in my crib. He came home when Walter Cronkite would be on the television. He would pick me up and play with me and hold me in his arms. I remember it like yesterday.

Now my dad is dead. We were very close. We lived together with my amazing wife. My parents gave me gifts that I could never repay. My life has been a whirlwind. Everything that I have written about is true.

It takes a great deal of courage to open yourself up to the world. The fact is that I have made a bunch of mistakes in my life. Fallacies make me even more special. To live the life of a square and a circle at the same time. To be a nerd and a jock. To be rich and poor, tall and short. Smart and dumb all in the same life. To be a walking paradox. High and sober again.

I was a Catholic baby, baptized early as a little boy before I left Greenville, Mississippi. I would bang my head on the concrete. Why am I telling you all of this? Because I do not have anything to hide. Because our strength comes from our failures. We must learn to reveal our own fallacies. I have always learned more from the mistakes I made than from what I did right.

When I was a little boy, I got burned by the iron and I did not do that again. Many years later, when I was a young adult, I almost died from alcohol poisoning. I didn't do that again. Many people have been in a drunken stupor from alcohol, but went back for more later that week. I quit drinking because of my diabetes. I quit doing drugs because it almost killed me several times. Drugs scared me straight.

I flunked out of school several times. It took me a while to realize that I was banging my head on the curb again. What was I doing wrong? Everything! It takes some people more time than others to learn what is bad for them.

Letters of Love to the World from a Dark Man

I had the same problem with women, but to a lesser degree. I must admit, for the most part, if I broke up with a woman, it was over. I learned that whatever broke you up the first time will break you up again. That's why I very seldom ever tried to go back to the same woman I broke up with.

I thought of myself as being a coward. Some days I wouldn't even go to class to take the test because I was high and couldn't pass the test. If you don't have the courage to try, then you are a failure. It takes more courage to fail than not to try at all.

Later in life, I learned what my mother was trying to teach me all along. She told me that you have to study like you're failing. The goal is to get 100% on the test—not an A, but 100%. My mother was a straight-A student. She received her doctorate in education.

A friend of mine in nursing school expounded on the subject. He said that in nursing and medical professions, we should all be 100% on everything. Because if you are a 70% nurse or doctor, that means that you are making a mistake three out of 10 times. This increases the chances that you can hurt someone. By making three mistakes, you may kill someone. I changed my paradigm.

Charles Clark

We can only strive for perfection. Perfection is left unto God. God is perfect. We strive to be perfect people. At this time when diseases are running rampant, the safety of people is paramount. God put diseases, war, famine, and natural disasters into motion on a grand scale to show us that he is in control. We need to turn to him for answers. We need to spend more time with our families and loved ones, reflecting on life and God.

Power is the ability to control people, plain and simple. You don't have to have money to have power.

Racism is stupid because all people are the same race—the human race.

Religion is a belief system that brings you closer to God. The God that you believe in. The goal of religion is for you to become like the God you worship. For those who do not believe in anything, what do you become?

The Bible is the number one selling book in the world every year. Why do they sell so many copies? What's the book about? The book is a history book and a reference book. Why ask why?

Prejudice is according to the things we know and the people we meet. We must always keep our hearts and minds open to God. We can only receive a blessing when our hearts and minds are open to everyone. You never know who God is going to use to bless you. A complete stranger of a different race, creed, or color could bless you. Love everyone!

Sex is a gift from God to procreate a bundle of joy, not a hedonistic goal of an orgasm.

Violence is a struggle. The struggle is real. Animals eat other animals to survive. People have misused our resource system since the beginning of time.

Money is nothing, but in our world today it is a necessary evil. We have to pay for resources to survive. The lack of money increases violence.

Love is God, and God is love. We have to start by loving ourselves in order to love anyone else. Love God and everything else will fall in line.

War is a money machine put on by the powers that be in order to fatten their pockets. Let the politicians be cannon fodder. They send our young people to fight a war that these fat cats arranged but do not fight in. Next time, let the politicians fight the wars and let the soldiers stay home. A fist fight to the death.

Family is the fundamental unit of any society. Love your family. Show me a child who is disrespectful to their parents and I will show you someone who will disrespect you too. If you will cuss out your mama, what do you think you have for me?

Drugs are wonderful. Many people take prescription drugs to live, me being one of them. Drugs are not bad, but the abuse of them is bad. Alcohol is a drug—a strong drug. All abuse is bad. Do what you're supposed to do to remain healthy: take your prescribed medications.

Hate is the opposite of love. There are people in the world who believe that hate and love are one and the same. A person who hates to lose loves to win. Do you exhibit good sportsmanship when you lose? Does your hate turn into violence? Do you hate yourself? Hate starts at home when you hate yourself. Love yourself instead.

Life is over before you know it. The brevity of life should drive us all. We are given this present on earth to find our purpose. What is the purpose of your life? Can you answer that question? God knows!

Death is a door. When one door closes, another door opens. Everybody wants to go to heaven, but nobody wants to die. It is coming, so get your house in order. If we knew the hour of our death, would we live our lives differently? Probably so. We would accomplish more, I guess.

God has all the answers. God created us, but some people believe that we created God.

Go out and love someone. Did you love someone today?